BEDSIDE COACHING

7 Lessons of Empowerment

SOPHIA PETRIDES
&
RAYMOND AARON

 AuthoritiesPress

Bedside Coaching™: 7 Lessons of Empowerment

www.petrides.consulting

Copyright © 2020 Sophia Petrides

ISBN: 979-8606768462

Publisher
10-10-10 Publishing
Markham, ON
Canada

Printed in the United Kingdom, the United States and Canada.

Dedication

I dedicate this book to all my readers across the globe. With this book, may you find inner inspiration and empowerment to spark a transformation in your lives!

Table of Contents

Table of Contents

Acknowledgements

I would like to thank my mother and late father for the wisdom, guidance, and unconditional love they have given me throughout my life. Without them, I would not have been able to grow and develop into the person that I am today, and for this, I am most grateful to them!

I give thanks to my brother, sister and to my beautiful nieces for their love and for being very supportive in many aspects of my life.

Over the years, I have been blessed with incredible friendships and mentors. I would like to give thanks to all those who have touched my life and have been with me throughout the good times and challenging times.

I am most grateful and give thanks to the universe and my "angels," who have been my constant companions, protecting me from negative influences, giving me encouragement and fierce courage to step into the unknown with certainty, and giving me inner strength and tenacity to manage my challenges head-on, and to take risks and never give up.

Foreword

Having been a successful coach myself for over 50 years, and having trained over 300,000 people around the world, I can attest to the power of having help from an expert.

Creating change and fostering growth in your life takes effort; however, no matter who you are, doubt can set in from time to time. *Bedside Coaching: 7 Lessons of Empowerment* is a powerful source of motivation to keep you moving forward, using coaching to achieve your goals and create your dream life.

Right from the start, Sophia Petrides shares her experience with coaching and its benefits. Each lesson in *Bedside Coaching* starts with a coaching discussion of the topic and includes multiple coaching tasks along the way. Then Sophia gives you space to write your thoughts and set your own goals, based on that Bedside Coaching topic.

Along the way, Sophia coaches you through each topic, giving you small bites to cover during a few minutes of your time daily. Plus, *Bedside Coaching* gives you the ability to go back and revisit different coaching points as you move through the book. With her years of leading and coaching people, Sophia covers critical points in a fresh way, to give you a new perspective. From self-awareness to emotional intelligence, Sophia's coaching is meant to motivate and inspire you to achieve growth and take risks.

Sophia Petrides

Don't set a goal for your personal life or professional career without taking advantage of your Bedside Coach!

Marcia Martin
CEO, Power of Speaking Seminars
www.marciamartin.com

Introduction

Coaching is a key part of my life, and it is how I have found personal and professional success. It is a process that helps you get into the mentality of continual improvement. However, working with a coach on a one-to-one basis can sometimes be difficult to fit into your busy schedule. Still, it is a process that helps you to prioritise your dreams and your goals, making it worth the effort to buy out the time.

With that in mind, I decided to look at how we can create a coaching habit, making it part of our self-care. The most successful individuals I know take that time to care for themselves, physically, mentally, emotionally, and spiritually. It involves recharging ourselves, allowing us to tap into those reserves when we really need them.

Now let's think about your self-care routine. I am sure that you have a specific morning routine, one that may already involve exercise or meditation before you begin your day. It helps you to get into the right frame of mind to tackle the challenges of the day. The same may be said for your routine before going to bed. You might do some relaxing meditation, pray, or another aspect of your spiritual routine. Perhaps part of your bedtime routine involves a journal about the day, allowing you to express your thoughts and give a voice to any joys or frustrations.

Those routines are critical to helping you maintain your balance and self-care in a life that can be full of stress and anxiety, which is constantly tugging on you to be present with your family, with your children, with your work, and with yourself. Within that mix, there is often little focus on how to make changes to improve various areas of your life. Coaching is a way to access tips and experience, to give you the tools to improve.

Finding time to take advantage of coaching can be difficult. In a traditional coaching session, you have to schedule an appointment and try to carve out time in an already busy day. Clearly, it is easy to see how coaching can be pushed to the side by other priorities. There does not seem to be enough time in the day!

I would argue that coaching is a critical part of your self-care, and that neglecting it can mean constantly leaving your batteries less than fully charged.

We are meant to be continuously learning and growing. When you neglect that aspect of your life, it can drag you down in a variety of ways.

My goal with *Bedside Coaching* is to help you incorporate coaching into your daily routine. These chapters are short, so they can easily be read before going to bed. Plus, you can also take advantage of the opportunity to review chapters as necessary. You can write down goals and ideas, using them throughout the next day, and then evaluate how you did the next evening. You also have the added benefit of refocusing your mind from the negative aspects of the day and turning toward positive ones. Falling asleep with a positive mindset can help you sleep better and leave you feeling more refreshed to tackle the next day.

I believe that all of us need encouragement, and not only that, we need to be challenged! *Bedside Coaching* is about challenging you to make constant improvements in your life and giving you the tools to do so. Understand that you have the capacity to achieve so much that your dreams and goals do not have to remain mental pictures or thoughts. They can become your reality; however, you need to be open to the possibilities.

I challenge you to spend a few minutes each evening with *Bedside Coaching*.

The purpose of this book is to outline key lessons to support you by creating a permanent feeling of empowerment within. I would like this book—hence the title, *Bedside Coaching*—to be used as your personal diary, and to be kept next to your bed as a constant companion in your life. This will keep you focused, ensuring your goals are kept alive and refreshed on a regular basis, so that you do not lose sight of the "bigger picture" in your life. It will support you on a daily basis and provide you with reminders of how you should live your life.

Following each chapter, you will notice a blank page called "Readers Notes." I recommend you put these pages into good use by writing down your thoughts, so that you can start shaping your goals. Following my instructions on how to create your goals, I have added a few pages so that you can clearly outline these and start making the necessary adjustments throughout the timeline you have allocated in achieving these. I have also included coaching tasks to help you focus on an area, and to stimulate growth.

The same process can be repeated to help you outline your "Life Purpose." As you take advantage of *Bedside Coaching*, you may see that there are areas you want to explore more deeply. I also offer coaching on a one-to-one basis, either in person, Skype or Zoom, and you can also attend my bespoke retreats and masterclasses.

Visit my website at **www.petrides.consulting** to take advantage of a free sample coaching session, and book your session today.

Build personal coaching into your daily routine...and develop the healthy habits of self-improvement, so let's start this journey together!

Bedside Coaching #1 – Live Aware

Many individuals equate self-awareness with a touchy-feely type of mantra about finding yourself after being lost. You might even be wondering how self-awareness applies to you. After all, you are not lost! You are in the comfort of your bed, relaxing before drifting off to sleep.

Self-awareness is defined as focusing our attention on ourselves, evaluating and comparing our behaviour to our internal standards and values. We are essentially becoming objective self-evaluators. This involves more than just accumulating knowledge about ourselves. Self-awareness includes paying attention to our inner state with a beginner's mind and an open heart. It allows us to be aware of the conditioning and preconceptions that are part of our lives, thus allowing us to make conscious choices to counteract those effects.

The practice of self-awareness is one of the greatest skills in life, because you are learning about yourself in a way that goes beyond anything anyone else could teach you. It involves self-control and emotional awareness. You learn who you are and how that translates into how you interact with others.

The most important aspect is awareness. That involves paying attention. There are so many daily events that we may not even consciously be aware of, simply because they do not have our focus and attention. Your consciousness is actively gathering and processing information from your daily environment, and then piecing it together with information that was gathered in the past. It is how you experience life, and how you reference and give importance to various events or surroundings.

Perhaps you may find yourself at an office meeting, and what you glean from the information presented might be different than what your colleague takes away from the same meeting. Why? Because there is a lot of information coming at us constantly, and our brains are wired to pick and choose what to focus on. You might find yourself hyperaware of a particular part of an event, while a friend might notice completely different details because their focus is broader.

Neither is right or wrong; however, it is an example of how our natural tendencies can come to the forefront when it comes to what our consciousness acknowledges and focuses on. Clearly, we can be aware of our surroundings, but it is important that we also spend time focusing our awareness on ourselves.

Self-awareness is the ability that you have to notice your feelings, your physical sensations, your reactions, your habits, your behaviour, and your thoughts, as if they were part of a scene that you were observing. You become the third-party observer of your own life, as well as of your internal thoughts and processes.

Self-image is often wrapped up in how we want others to perceive us, not necessarily how we perceive ourselves. It can be easy to believe that people see us one way, when in fact, the reality of our situation is entirely different. As part of your journey to become more self-aware, you will need to consciously focus on the reality of your behaviour and not the story you may tell yourself about who you are and how you behave.

Part of true self-awareness is the ability to be honest with ourselves about the choices we make and the actions that we take. That is not always easy to do! As humans, we tend to be much harsher on others than we are on ourselves. Do you find yourself calling others out regarding their behaviour, but quick with excuses or extenuating circumstances for your own actions?

Self-awareness involves standing up and acknowledging the impact of your actions on yourself and others. It means claiming them without excuses or justification for your actions.

Many of us claim that we are honest and tell others *straight* what they need to hear, but we get hurt or offended if others were to do the same to us. Honesty with ourselves means acknowledging when we are making an excuse to dismiss our actions or justify them. After all, we all have control over our actions, even if we cannot control our circumstances or the actions of others.

Your Coaching Task:

Take one recent action that impacted another individual. Why did you choose that particular action? When you look at that action, do you find yourself creating excuses? What type of excuses are you creating? By acknowledging your excuses and justifications, you can begin to determine what thought processes caused you to make them in various situations.

Once you acknowledge your thought process, you can then begin the process of shifting them.

Exploring Your Feelings

Going into your journey of self-awareness involves not only being honest with yourself about the reasons for your actions, but also being honest about your feelings. I have met many individuals who feel as if their life is on autopilot and the scenery never changes. On the surface of your life, everything may appear fine, however, there is a feeling that something is not right.

Without self-awareness, it can be easy to simply ignore that feeling or suppress it. Self-awareness involves exploring those unexplained feelings, instead of simply pushing them away. Those unexplained feelings can end up having physical manifestations, such as a knot in the pit of your stomach or tingling in your chest. You might recognise that you feel unhappy or unsatisfied; however, you are unsure as to the reason why.

How can you begin the process of exploring your feelings? Start by not ignoring the feelings. Instead, make it a point to notice the circumstances where they seem the strongest. What is going on? What are you thinking about? Exploring your feelings involves turning off your internal conscious chatter for a moment and, instead, give a voice to your feelings.

Exploring the unknown can be scary. You might be worried that you will uncover something you have been ignoring or blocking from your consciousness. It could even be a trauma or past events that you have pushed away. However, those feelings are going to keep coming back until you address them. Exploring what triggers them, or the roots of those feelings, can involve coming to a deeper understanding of what makes you tick and what frustrates or upsets you. At the very least, exploring your feelings allows you to learn more about who you are and how to live in closer alignment with yourself.

Once you identify the circumstances or thoughts that are causing your feelings, you can then take action to address these. Often, if you are feeling a sense of dissatisfaction in your life, you may need to make changes, which could include setting new goals, re-evaluating relationships, or perhaps adjusting your viewpoint regarding where you are in your life.

It can be easy to get so caught up in what we wish our lives to be, that we forget the power we have to create the life we dreamed of. I want you to see self-awareness as a tool to help you determine where you want to go and how you want to get there. As you come into a deeper understanding of who you are, then you can determine what your goals are, based on what is important to you instead of what is important to others.

Your Coaching Task:

Identify a feeling that may have been with you throughout the day. When did the feeling start? Can you remember what was happening when it started? Were you reacting to the actions of others? Was it a point of self-disappointment, because you did not achieve a goal?

Identifying the events surrounding your feeling can lead you to a deeper understanding of yourself, and why those events brought that specific feeling to the surface.

Practicing Self-Awareness

Becoming aware of your emotions is one of the critical steps to greater self-awareness. Depending on your social and cultural upbringing, you may have been taught that emotions are not to be part of your decision making. In fact, you might believe that decisions should only be made based on our rational thoughts.

The truth is that our emotions do impact our decisions, even if we might not wish to acknowledge that reality. When we try to ignore them, it means that our decision-making process gets out of alignment. Too often, our rational decisions are based on what others expect of us, and we end up trying to live according to someone else's ideals, be it our parents, a significant other, our culture, or even our social environment.

Your feelings, on the other hand, are your way of advocating for yourself. To make the best decisions, we need to acknowledge that internal advocate—our feelings—as well as those outside influences that impact our rational thoughts. Listen to your gut! You may find that you need to explore why your feelings object so strongly to a decision made through rational thought.

The first step is to acknowledge your feelings and to ask yourself where they come from. The next step looks at tracking your feelings. Journaling can be a great way to start noticing patterns and trends.

When you are monitoring your feelings, you are essentially communicating with your subconscious, which is your true inner voice. Often, that inner voice knows what you want out of life before you are able to put it into words.

Your Coaching Task:

Start writing down your positive feelings and your negative feelings. Keep them in a journal or create a note on your phone, tablet, or digital assistant. You might even note down a sentence or two about what was going on at the time, and the time of day that the feeling occurred.

You are going to start seeing patterns and trends emerge. Those patterns can help you to see and define your values, your motivations, and anything that might be holding you back from fulfilling your purpose or the work that you want to do. If you are having trouble finding your purpose, you may begin to notice the pattern of things that bring you joy and the activities that do not.

This work can help you to define your purpose and give you a direction to start moving toward, which will allow you to fulfill it.

Expanding Self-Awareness Beyond Your Feelings

It is important to recognise that the skills you are gaining, relating to self-awareness of your emotions, can be used in other areas of your life. This expansion should start in areas that can have the greatest impact on designing your ideal lifestyle. For instance, tracking your feelings about your professional life might help you to design a path to make changes that can bring you closer to what you want to achieve professionally as it relates to your purpose.

Once you have a handle on tracking your feelings and putting the information to use in making your decisions, you can start to expand that tracking to include your energy. Essentially, when you are tracking your energy, you are looking to find the time of day in which you perform your best. These periods of the day are when you feel *on point*—essentially, when you are the most productive, energetic, and focused. During these times of the day, you are likely to be the most creative, and produce your best work.

Think about how people might refer to themselves as morning people or night owls. The truth is that they are identifying peak periods of energy that they may have noticed over the years. Now, that doesn't mean that if you are a night owl, you are not going to have to get up in the morning and head to a job. Instead, knowing that your peak creativity and energy is in the evening, can help you to find opportunities in your professional career to match up to those times.

Working as a contractor or freelancer can be a great way to set a schedule that works around those times of optimal energy.

Tracking your energy can also help identify what drains you physically, emotionally, mentally, and spiritually. It could be circumstances or people that leave you feeling drained and frustrated. You might not be able to avoid them altogether; however, understanding that they are draining can help you to find ways to limit their impact on your energy whenever possible.

You are also going to find out which people and circumstances motivate you. You can take that information and use it to increase their presence in your life. Motivation can help you to keep moving forward in achieving a goal or a dream, as part of your life's purpose, even when it becomes challenging.

Throughout this chapter, I have given you some coaching tasks. I want you to use these as exercises that can help you to build your self-awareness. Feel free to come back and revisit them from time to time. Taking the time to increase your self-awareness is going to help you understand your feelings better, and also help you to relieve your anxiety and stress.

You are taking the time to learn about your needs and desires. Doing so will help you in crafting your plan for the future.

Your Coaching Task:

Track your energy for 30 days. Note the times when you felt energised, when you felt creative, and when you were motivated. Jot down a few thoughts about the circumstances. After 30 days, you will start to see patterns. Begin to use those patterns to increase your productivity.

Self-awareness is a key step on the path to achieving your dreams and purpose in order to build your ideal life.

Being in the Right Consciousness

Part of self-awareness involves recognising more about the *why* and *what* of your choices and actions, instead of just focusing on identifying your personal strengths and areas of development. After all, when you understand the *why* and *what*, then it makes it easier for you to focus on making changes to address where you need to develop or to capitalise on strengths.

Another important aspect of understanding the *why* and *what* is the motivation that they can provide when dealing with challenges on the way to achieving a specific goal or desire.

Your Coaching Task:

Pick a specific goal and then write about the reasons behind that goal. Then ask yourself questions such as:

- Is this particular goal motivated by what I think I should aim for, or by expectations of others?

- How does it align with who I am as a person, my beliefs, and what I value?

- What do I hope to accomplish for myself and others by achieving this goal?

As you can see, all these questions are about exploring the *why* and *what* behind your goals, and the choices you make to achieve them. Clearly, the more self-aware you are, the better you will be able to see how your *why* and *what* line up with your goals.

To discover the *why* and *what*, you need to be open to asking yourself deeper questions, looking more deeply at the reasons and thoughts behind your actions. It involves being honest about those reasons.

We all have moments when we find it easier to blame others or the circumstances, instead of digging deeper within ourselves. Embracing self-awareness helps you to understand the judgements that you are making of others.

Often, we tend to judge others harshly because we see things in them that mirror ourselves. Take the time to reflect on what I just said: "We tend to judge others because we see things in them that mirror ourselves." If you are open to taking responsibility and accountability of your judgements, and not judge others, you are truly on the way of achieving self-awareness.

The motives that we attach to the actions of others, often might reflect our own motives. Self-awareness is not just learning about yourself; it is also learning about how you interact with others and why you interact with them in that manner.

This is an ongoing process, and I want to be clear that you are courageous by opening your mind and heart to this self-exploration.

Failure does not mean that you have failed! Unfortunately, many of us have internalised failure as a commentary about who we are as individuals. Self-awareness is about separating the two and processing the failure as a teaching moment, instead of a commentary about your character and who you are.

With that in mind, remember that focusing on the now can be a pivotal part of moving beyond failure, into a greater level of understanding and personal growth.

Looking for help to understand the lessons resulting from your failures? Visit my website at **www.petrides.consulting** to book a free sample coaching session today!

Sophia Petrides

Readers Notes

Readers Notes

Sophia Petrides

Readers Notes

Bedside Coaching #2 – Live Now

As you become more self-aware, you generate a deeper understanding of yourself and how you interact with others. Too often, we tend to focus on the future planning, thinking about a time when we will finally be able to do everything that we imagined. In the process, we completely turn away from focusing on the present time.

Yet by focusing so much on what possibilities the future contains, we are actually missing out on the opportunity to shape our future by the choices we make in the present time. Essentially, the opportunities you take advantage of today are going to be the ones that impact your future. When you choose not to act now, for whatever reasons, then you are essentially limiting your future.

Part of the process of shaping your future starts with recognising how the choices that you are making (or not making) are impacting your ability to achieve your dreams. In Bedside Coaching #1, I focused on helping you get to know yourself and become self-aware. The next step is to understand where you want to go. When you have a better understanding of yourself and your dreams, then you can create a roadmap to help you get where you want to go.

By Living Now, I want you to start the process of defining your future by shaping your present. It starts with your big dream or major life purpose.

What is Your Life Purpose?

I want you to stop for a moment. Close your eyes and take a few deep breaths. What do you see when you think about your ideal life? What are you doing with your days? How are you impacting others? Try and give that picture as much detail as possible. The point is to make your future life as real as possible in your head. If you do, then you will have a clear picture of what you want to create in your physical reality.

Your Coaching Task:

Define your dream life and write about it in your journal. Give it plenty of details. As you do, make a point to stop and meditate on that dream or goal. Make it a part of your daily routine to dwell on it, and even refine the details. Make a sharp and clear picture in your head.

Now that you have a clear vision of your dream life, it is time to start looking for the milestones or mini goals that will allow you to achieve that dream. The reason behind this, is that it can be overwhelming to achieve any large goal or dream, as you see it to be a massive task in front of you. Once you break it down into smaller tasks, you now have a way to measure your progress and make it easier to understand how you are going to achieve that large goal.

Goal setting is key to any endeavour that you undertake. If you want to be successful, you need small goals or milestones to help you judge your progress. Those milestones can also help you to find opportunities that can propel you forward.

The fact is that our brains are going to focus on whatever we spend the most time thinking about. If you are focusing on your goals, then your subconscious is going to be looking for people and experiences that will help you to achieve those goals. It becomes part of your day-to-day activities. You will be amazed at how much you can achieve when you make goals and then focus on them daily.

What is the First Step?

With the goal in mind, start writing down milestones or the steps that you feel you need to achieve in order to accomplish the goal. This is not a right or wrong answer. You may write down as many steps or milestones as you feel are necessary to get the job done.

Once you note them down, it is important to look for that natural first step. What is the first thing that you can do today to start you down the path of achieving your goal? It could be as simple as signing up for a class or contacting a mentor. You might want to read a book on a topic related to your larger goal, growing your knowledge base.

Other people find that their first step is even more action oriented and requires them to put themselves out there and build up their network. Whatever that first step is, you need to make it your goal for today. Do not wait until tomorrow. The point is that you want to shape your future starting right now.

With that first step accomplished, define the next step. Remember, the point is to build on what you have already accomplished. It could be working on taking a risk or making changes to your finances to give you the freedom to explore other career opportunities. The point is that with each step, you take yourself further down the path toward achieving your goal.

Your Coaching Task:

Make a list of milestones related to your dream or big goal. Then pick one to make part of your day's activities.

Part of this coaching task is about forming a new habit. If you take a step toward your goal each day, no matter how small, you are using "Live Now" to shape your future.

Milestones Are Stepping Stones

Understand that each milestone is just a stepping stone to your larger goal. You are going to find that you can even break down milestones into smaller goals. As you are defining milestones, you need to see them as a measurement tool. Too often, we ignore the progress we have made, simply because they are just small steps forward. Life and society tend to make us believe that progress can only be achieved if it comes in dramatic changes or large shifts in our lives.

In the process, we are hard on ourselves, simply because we feel that we haven't made enough progress. That means we are discounting all the progress that we have made. You can end up discouraging yourself to the point that you give up.

I want you to recognise that your progress is critical to keeping you empowered and motivated by achieving your big dreams and goals. When you tend to focus in a negative way on the small steps, then you derail the growth of your motivation.

Building motivation starts with acknowledging that your daily habits need to change. Getting stuck is easy to do, however, having a habit that requires you to do something every day to move you closer to a goal, is going to keep you from feeling stuck. You are going to find that you are working harder, because those daily tasks are helping to create progress. Your present is being shifted, and that is impacting your future, even if you can't see it right now.

Your Coaching Task:

Identify small milestones that can be accomplished on a daily basis. Start your day by reminding yourself what is possible that day. Check back on the progress you have made so far, allowing it to motivate you as a new day begins.

Altering Your Viewpoint to Find Opportunities

Another aspect of shifting your present to create your future is being open to opportunities. Right now, I am going to talk about taking risks, particularly those related to achieving a dream or large goal. Risks are simply opportunities that present themselves. You might not be 100% happy of the outcome from that opportunity, and by taking that risk, then you are opening yourself up to new possibilities.

Part of the way that you can build toward achieving your dreams is by changing your viewpoint regarding risk. If you are not willing to take risks, then you are going to cut yourself off from critical opportunities that may support you reaching that end goal. Your viewpoint of risk needs to be open to failure and learning from your mistakes. If your viewpoint is one that negatively focuses on risk, you become risk adverse. You may see failure as invalidating your dream, making it unworthy of your continued efforts.

Here is the reality: failure just means that a particular way did not work, and now you have to try another way.

The men and women who made history did not find success on their first try. In fact, many of them failed multiple times. Best-selling authors had their works rejected. Entrepreneurs talk about failure on many occasions, and the number of times they have lost money, only to find success with just one of their business plans. Failure is part of the growth and learning process. If you do not embrace risk, then you cannot embrace failure and learn.

When you shift your viewpoint, and welcome failure, then you are also opening your mind to opportunities. You might find yourself being exposed to an idea or process that can help you take a giant leap forward in achieving your dream or goal.

Your viewpoint is often impacted by what types of thoughts you allow yourself to dwell on. Is your self-talk focused on how things are not going to work out? If so, then you are talking yourself out of what could be truly amazing, and actually helping to create a life of being stuck and frustrated.

Your Coaching Task:

What is a negative thought that you regularly have? Write down a positive version, one that allows you to shift your viewpoint in that particular area. As you find yourself shifting your thoughts, it can begin to help you embrace risk and failure, because you can see them differently.

Take the Time to Just "Be"

Shifting your thoughts involves allowing time for you to simply *be*. In this case, it means being alone with your thoughts or giving yourself time to simply turn your mind off and just breathe in the beauty of the moment. Too often, our lives move at such a fast pace, making it hard to create change that will impact our future.

I want you to make it a daily part of your life to stop and breathe. It can be hard to determine your direction in the frenzy of everyday life. By scheduling time to just *be*, you are acknowledging the importance of stepping away from the chaos of your life. Doing so, can also help you to recharge and even refocus on your vision for your future, or even on a particular project you are working on.

How can you just *be*? Start by finding a quiet spot or time of day when you can just be alone with your thoughts. Many take walks as part of this time, simply because it allows them to connect with nature and how their bodies move and interact with their environment. Learning to just *be* can involve simply taking the time to appreciate how your breath moves in and out of your lungs.

Connecting with nature is an important part of the process. The beauty of our universe is a source of inspiration. During this time, you can clear your mind and use it to help you reset. When you are worried and upset about something, it can cloud your mind, and that can limit your possibilities or even how you view opportunities.

By clearing your mind, it allows you to stop the process of worrying and fretting. You are putting the brakes on a spiral of negative thinking. You can't remove the chaos and fears from your life if you are allowing them to negatively impact your thinking. Taking time to stop can allow you to get control of that chaos within your mind, which then translates into controlling the chaos in your physical life.

To permanently remove your chaos and fears, it requires you opening your mind to new possibilities and experiences.

Self-awareness is not just about understanding where you want to go; it is also understanding how you think, knowing your goals, and then putting habits into place that will help you to support and achieve these goals and dreams. When you focus on what you are doing right now, then you are going to positively impact your future.

Your Coaching Task:

Find a place that speaks to your mind and soul, a place where you can be quiet and just *be*. Make it a habit to spend time in that space on a daily basis. Doing so can help you to reconnect with yourself and to also reconnect with your body and your environment.

Readers Notes

Sophia Petrides

Readers Notes

Bedside Coaching #3 – Live Values

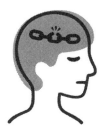

Part of your journey is defining what guides and motivates you, which is often referred to as your values. The world defines values as the basic and fundamental principles, serving as your foundation, guiding and motivating your thoughts and actions. You determine the values and beliefs that you will live by, but at the same time, it is critical to be aware of your values, and to be open to adjusting those underlying beliefs when necessary.

Your experiences are going to inform your beliefs, thus shaping your values. Therefore, examining your beliefs is important to make sure that your values reflect who you are now, instead of functioning on values that no longer fit your beliefs.

Those same values help you to decide what is important to you, and they guide you to define your priorities. They often inform the type of person that you want to be, and the life purpose that you want to pursue.

Part of understanding yourself better, as discussed in Bedside Coaching #1, is the importance of understanding the underlying beliefs that fuel your values. We are now going to explore a breakdown of various values and their meanings, as well as how important it is to live by these values. First, let's explore how values and ethics go hand in hand.

Values Inform Ethics

Values are often associated with what is good, desirable, or worthwhile. Personal values are based on your personal belief system and what you believe is right and wrong, even if it is not considered moral by society or the majority. Cultural values are often defined as the values accepted by religions or societies, reflecting what each of them finds important, particularly as it relates to content.

Ethics, on the other hand, are concerned not only with human actions but also with how you choose those actions. It is part of a continual evaluation of the choices we make, and also the values that underlie those choices.

In fact, you may find that your ethics determine what values you pursue, and the ones that you opt not to. At the same time, if you value something, then you are willing to stand up for that value, instead of just allowing others to dictate their actions. With strong values, you are going to be able to stand up to strong condemnation from others. Your values can help you to be a leader, or they can put you in the position of being a follower, one who tends to be driven by the prevailing winds of the current cultural environment.

When it comes to understanding your values, you need to recognise how they inform the choices you make, and your moral code that governs your actions. Remember, what you value may not be the same as what someone else values. Your values are going to be specific to your relationships and your goals; however,

36

it still has a rational aspect. Here is a simple way to illustrate that point.

A person who values honesty might be a whistleblower on financial wrongdoing by a superior. On the other hand, a person who values loyalty highly could be silent regarding that same wrongdoing. As you can see, values can conflict, especially between individuals who have different values and beliefs.

As you mature in life, your values may stand up to the test of time, meaning that they are always indicative of good and rightful behaviour. To truly understand your values, you have to distinguish between those intrinsic values—ones that are values in their own right—versus extrinsic values, which are usually motivated by something else, such as wealth or fame.

Your Coaching Task:

List a few of your core values, perhaps focusing on the beliefs that helped you to formulate those values. Ask yourself the following questions regarding each of the values on your list:

- Why is this value important to me?

- How does it help me to prioritise my actions and life choices?

- Are my values falling in line with my beliefs, or are they being influenced by outside forces?

Now that you have an idea of what your own values are, let's start exploring a few key values and how they can impact you.

Value #1 – Integrity

According to Merriam-Webster, integrity is defined as *"a firm adherence to a code of especially moral or artistic values, incorruptibility; an unimpaired condition, soundness; the quality or state of being complete or undivided, completeness."* This is a word that you hear on a daily basis; however, the question is, how can it truly impact your life? Simply put, for many individuals, the root of integrity is about doing the right thing even when it is not something that others can see or comment on, and even when it is not convenient to you.

This value is what I consider a key to avoiding an indulgence in self-interest at the expense of others around you. I am sure that as you meditate on it, you can think of several instances where integrity played a part in your life or the lives of others.

If you are a parent for instance, you can show integrity in how you deal with your children. If you make a mistake and apologise to them, then you show them your integrity, and you also help them to learn how to show integrity in their own lives.

If you are a boss, then it can be easy to take credit for the work that your employees have completed, or for their ideas. However, integrity means that you give credit where credit is due, even if it means downplaying your own accomplishments. It helps others to see you as a respected leader, one that gives credit for their contributions.

In your romantic relationships, integrity might involve making the conscious decision not to fight unfairly, but instead to use humanity and kindness, even during an argument. That means no name calling or below-the-belt behaviour. It involves being willing to control your emotional impulses, even when no one else but your partner is around to see your actions.

These are just a few situations where integrity can come into play. I am sure that you can think of others!

Your Coaching Task:

Take a moment to think of an area of your life, or a particular situation, where you had to make a decision that no one would know about. Meditate on the meaning of integrity, and then do an honest self-examination. Ask yourself:

- Did I make a decision that was easier for me, potentially at the expense of my integrity?

- How did I display integrity?

- Is there a way that I could display integrity in that type of situation to a greater degree?

Value #2 – Authenticity

For many of us, authenticity is a value and quality that is highly prized. We value those around us who are genuine and original, even when it goes against the crowd. According to Merriam-Webster, authenticity is defined as *"worthy of acceptance or belief as conforming to or based on fact; not false or imitation; true to one's own personality, spirit, or character."*

At the same time, you might know people that are quick to point out what is *phony* or *false* in someone else. While in theory, we all want to avoid such people, it can be hard to avoid your own self.

Authenticity is more than being passionate about what you believe, and speaking out, even if people do not want to hear it.

After all, someone can speak out and be passionate in line with their beliefs, but not be authentic. True authenticity is focused around demonstrating a psychological maturity, which allows you to establish a few of the following:

- Realistic perceptions of reality, even if it is not always in your favour.

- Accepting yourself and others for who and what you/ they are.

- Being thoughtful.

- Having a non-hostile sense of humour, which means not offending others to get a laugh or elevate your own status.

- Be open to learning from your mistakes.

- Have a clear understanding of your motivations.

- Expressing your feelings clearly and freely to others without being aggressive.

Part of genuine authenticity is recognising that you are not going to be able to change others, however, you can still express yourself in a way that invites dialogue instead of conflict. It is about collaborating with others in a way that reflects an ability to function in the world without blaming, criticising, judging, or getting defensive about who we are and the choices we make.

Your Coaching Task:

Look at a recent disagreement you may have had with another individual. Evaluate your actions. Did you do any of the following?

- Cut them off.

- Attack them personally through name calling or attacks on their character.

- Misunderstand their motives, perhaps assuming the worst.

- Automatically judging them before hearing them out.

Part of being authentic is demonstrated in how we deal with others, even during times when we disagree or may feel hurt by their actions. As you can see, authenticity involves being true to who you are, while still embracing an approach of self-honesty and openness about others. It doesn't always mean changing your stance but acknowledging that the other person's stance is valid as well.

Value #3 – Respect

As a society, respect is valued highly. Often, it is associated with how we view others, holding them in high regard, as well as how we treat them. Respect is not limited to our interactions with others. It also applies to how we treat and value ourselves!

When you respect someone, you treat them in a manner that demonstrates their value. You acknowledge who they are and what they are doing, giving them credit for their actions and their impact on the community as a whole. As a society, respect is considered a critical part of dealing with others. However, it is also not considered an automatic action, as many individuals will point out.

Have you heard the expression, or one similar to it, "They haven't earned my respect!" It gets to the core of many inter-actions between individuals today. An attitude has evolved that seems to be based on the idea of not giving respect to others until they give it to you. Yet that is not how respect works. It is something that you need to demonstrate as part of your daily personality, because no one owes you respect until you earn it.

Respectful behaviour, both toward yourself and others, needs to be a critical part of how you act with yourself and others. That being said, respect can be withdrawn when a person demonstrates an attitude of disrespect. Still, I want to add a note of caution. When someone is disrespectful to you, and you still show them respect, then you are demonstrating the content of your character.

It shows respect for yourself when you choose to treat others with respect, despite their actions. When you value respect for yourself, then you can see the importance of extending it to others.

Your Coaching Task:

As you start your day, remind yourself to be open to what others bring to the table. Showing respect to others is a way to earn it for yourself.

- Focus on being polite and kind, and view situations without judgement.

- Be willing to be wrong.

- Avoid dumping on others just because you are having a bad day.

Value #4 – Family

This value is focused on those we have our first relationships with—our family members. When we bring our authentic selves into these relationships, then we can build those relationships up. Family relationships can be the ones that we make work, even when they are not always healthy, because a sense of loyalty is wrapped up in them.

When it comes to your family, it is important to remember that your loyalty and ties to them should not come at the expense of your own mental health and well-being. It can be very difficult to make the decision to step back from an unhealthy family relationship, but in the end, that move can allow you both to redefine your interactions with each other.

With time, our beliefs and values are impacted by our experiences, so your relationships are going to be impacted. Setting boundaries in our relationships with family members, and sticking to them, can help you to grow and still maintain those relationships in a healthy way. In coaching you through this value, my point is that family means different things to individuals, and often it is focused on those we are related to through blood or marriage. However, no relationship remains stagnant. They can all grow and change. Be open to that change.

Your Coaching Task:

Connect with a family member in a positive way, either through a kind gesture or an invitation to lunch. Listen with an open mind and heart by putting aside, for that period, past judgements and perceived slights. It could mean growth for your relationship in a meaningful way.

Value #5 – Ambition

Ambition can be either positive or negative. Those individuals who attribute negativity to ambition often do so because of past behaviours that fed ambition at the expense of others. In business, ambition is valued to boost your career. In your personal life, ambition is often the motivation that gives you direction, and helps you to work hard to achieve your goals and vision for your life.

Ambition is tied to the energy necessary to chase after your goals and dreams, no matter what the field of your life. Your ambition helps you to overcome challenges by using various strategies to grow and successfully meet those challenges. Being ambitious also cultivates your desire for transformation, which can be key to creating lasting change in your life.

Think about completing your education. It required ambition to implement strategies to keep you on track. Your desire to achieve that goal probably kept you going when you were dealing with difficult classes or struggling to understand various concepts.

Clearly, ambition can be a good thing; however, when it becomes excessive, then it can fuel negative choices in your interactions with others, essentially running them over. Ambition can often be associated with self-esteem. Too much or too little of either can negatively impact us and our relationships. It is a combination of ambition and ethics that is key to achieving your goals, while not hurting others in the process.

Your Coaching Task:

Ambition is a desire to win, to grow, and to change. It can lead to major transformations. Think of one thing in each of the areas below where you could increase your ambition:

- Relationships with friends.

- Your career.

- Building your business.

- Growing your network.

- Connecting with family.

Ambitious people can see the "bigger picture," identify potential flaws, and implement strategies and solutions to address them. While we each have our parameters for success, a lack of ambition can lead to stagnation, which can negatively impact your ability to achieve your goals and fulfill your life purpose.

Value #6 – Creativity

I have added this value because, in order to find solutions to any challenge, you need to be creative and open to possibilities. Negative thinking patterns can get us into a loop where we only tend to shut down possibilities, pointing out how they won't work, or finding all the things that could potentially go wrong.

When you focus on being creative, you tap into your imagination. I love brainstorming sessions, where you write down all the solutions, no matter how improbable they may seem. The point is not to censor yourself. Many solutions can be found among those that were considered impossible or improbable.

With that being said, I want you to focus on building your creativity. Tapping it can involve focusing on art or a hobby. Fueling your creative side can benefit you in so many ways. Think of those individuals who have built amazing businesses or products that have changed the way the world works.

They altered society because of their creativity, which involves a willingness to take risks and to think differently. Making creativity a part of your daily life is important, because it impacts your success. Here are a few ways to incorporate creativity and cultivate it:

- Keep a journal – Like brainstorming, the idea is not to censor yourself but to simply write. It can be a great way to allow your thoughts to flow—and who knows what direction that could take you in!

- Draw – The importance is not on whether you could sell your drawings or make it big in the art world, but on the act of creating itself. The purpose is discovery.

- Connecting with nature – Take a journal or your art outside. The colours and wildlife can prove to be a great inspiration.

- Incorporate movement – It can be as simple as taking a walk; doing so can help you to get the creative juices flowing. New ideas and thoughts can surface, just because you changed your surroundings and stretched your muscles.

- Be playful – Playing is not just for kids. Stretch your imagination through games and being goofy. You will be amazed at what happens next!

- Keep learning – Use questions and reading to feed your need to learn. It doesn't stop just because you finished education. There are so many online learning opportunities available, so take advantage of these.

Your Coaching Task:

Pick one of the ways to spark creativity, available from the list above, or find another that speaks to your personal joys. Then implement it into your daily routine. Set just a few minutes aside each day. It can be amazing how your creativity grows by allowing space for it in your day.

Throughout this *Bedside Coaching* chapter, I wanted to focus on values, particularly how they impact your life. You may have additional values that are part of your personal list. As you think about these, it is important to remember that your values are part of who you are, and they inform your thoughts and actions.

This is clearly not an exhaustive list, however, it gives you a point to start from and then build upon. It will help you to understand where you are in terms of expressing that value in various areas of your life, and to find aspects of your life where you might need to improve. Recognise that we are all a work in progress! You may find yourself in a position where you need to revisit these values from time to time, giving yourself a refresher course.

You might also find it helpful to do additional research on these and other values. Doing so can help you to imprint them even more on your mind and in your heart. I encourage you to take the time to choose a value to focus on daily. Think about what goes into that value and how you express it, in your professional and personal life. As you gain experience, you can serve as an example to others.

If you are struggling with defining your values and how they are impacting your life, visit my website at **www.petrides.consulting** to book one of my free sample coaching sessions.

One aspect of expressing values involves a deeper understanding of your emotional intelligence, which is the focus of our next Bedside Coaching.

Readers Notes

Sophia Petrides

Readers Notes

Bedside Coaching #4 – Live Intelligently

51

Emotional intelligence is the ability to identify and manage our own emotions, as well as those of other individuals we come in contact with daily. It includes three skills: emotional awareness, the ability to harness those emotions, and the ability to manage emotions. When it comes to harnessing your emotions, you also need to be able to apply them to various tasks, such as problem solving or creative thinking. Managing your emotions means regulating your emotions, and also being able to cheer or calm another individual.

Our emotional well-being can be influenced by our surroundings, so being tuned into your emotions and those of others can make you a better friend, parent, leader, or even romantic partner. The question is, how can you recognise this emotional intelligence in yourself and others? You may find that it is a skill you can develop, so if it feels that you are lacking in that area, never fear!

Actions Illustrate Emotional Intelligence

Actions speak louder than words! When it comes to understanding the emotions of others, you need to be able to interpret their actions for the emotional meanings. Emotional intelligence often begins when we start empathising with others, regardless of whether our interactions with them are at work or in our personal lives.

Think of a moment when you were having a bad day or were feeling just awful. Was there someone who seemed to step up and know exactly what you needed, to help you weather that storm? It is a simple example of emotional intelligence, and one that illustrates the point. When you are able to be that individual for someone else, you expand personally.

However, there are also moments when we do not show that emotional maturity, and our actions can reflect that. When we demonstrate a lack of emotional intelligence, our relationships can be one-dimensional, which makes it hard for you to support others and be open to receiving their support.

Our ability to deepen our relationships can often be reflected by our ability to empathise with others. It is an area where we can grow and connect on a deeper level with others and understand our own selves better. To truly live an authentic life, one with honesty and self-awareness, emotional intelligence is critical.

Your Coaching Task:

Spend a few minutes today, observing people and initiating contact with them, if the emotional cues seem to indicate that they need encouragement. The point is to focus on others while gaining a deeper understanding of how people use emotional signals to express their needs for support.

Journal your experiences. Reflect on how you felt throughout the process. Doing so, will help you to gain a deeper understanding of how your own empathy can impact others.

Understanding Social and Emotional Intelligence

Emotional and social intelligence tend to walk hand in hand. They both help you to navigate social and emotional situations. While many similarities between the two exist, they each can impact different areas of your life.

For instance, when I talk about emotional intelligence, I am talking about recognising and managing the emotions, and your emotional responses, within the present. After all, you can't predict what circumstances will occur in the future or how they will make you feel. Plus, you can't predict how others will feel emotionally in the future about their own circumstances or your actions.

Social intelligence, on the other hand, is focused more on the future. You use some of the same skills and abilities, however, the goal is to understand the feelings, personalities, and behaviours of yourself and others to hopefully end up with a positive outcome. Note that both of them require you to process various cues to understand the emotional and social responses of others. Yet this is where we can struggle from time to time, as our ability to process these cues can get derailed in the moment.

Too often, it can be easy to get wrapped up in how we feel, to the point that we tend to project our feelings onto others, evaluating their responses from that point of view. Part of developing your emotional and social intelligence is separating your feelings from the actions of others, allowing their actions to speak for themselves.

For you to shift away from that type of response, it is important to create habits that can kick in for you in any given situation. Part of that process is self-analysis, which I have discussed earlier in Bedside Coaching #1. As you analyze your responses to situations, you can start to put different tools into place.

For instance, taking a pause in a heated moment, before you respond. The more you do it, the easier it gets to stop and connect with your feelings, and then manage them effectively. Note that the point is to start building a different response mechanism, one that can help you to tap into your emotional and social intelligence.

Your Coaching Task:

Think about a particular situation where you recognised your feelings and then managed them effectively. Write about that time, focusing on the following:

- What steps did I take to effectively recognise and manage my emotional response?

- How did that impact the situation?

- Are there other steps or tools I need to develop?

- Looking back, did I interpret the social and emotional cues of those individuals involved in the situation?

When you take the time to isolate incidents and look for what you did well, plus where you might improve, then you can tap into your emotional and social intelligence, which is critical to your ability to function in the world.

The Benefits of Living Intelligently

I have explored a few of the aspects of emotional intelligence, which I believe are important to successfully build relationships with others. Throughout this discussion, the focus has been on how to improve in terms of building your emotional intelligence. Now I want to talk about the ways that you can benefit from developing your emotional intelligence.

1. Feelings

One key benefit is that you have social and self-awareness, and the ability to reflect on your emotional responses to various events. It helps you to understand your emotional strengths and weaknesses, and also what might be going on underneath the surface. Imagine how much easier it can be to deal with others when you have a greater understanding of your own emotional responses.

It also helps you to gain a deeper understanding of why you feel the way you do, tapping into past experiences that may have negatively influenced you, creating emotional triggers. All of us have those triggers, however, it can be difficult to get the core of what has caused those triggers. Being in touch with your emotions can be a critical step in addressing these.

2. Building in the Pause

Pausing is often the best tool that we have when it comes to difficult situations. It gives us a moment to collect our thoughts and access our feelings. Immediate responses often lead to regrets later, as you think about what you did and wish that you had handled it differently. Taking the pause allows us to handle it differently in the moment, and it is a skill that continues to serve you well as you grow your emotional intelligence.

3. Taking Control of Your Thoughts

Your thoughts are your ability to create and build in your life. What you think about, manifests in your reality. It is just that simple!

I want you to recognise that emotional intelligence gives you the benefit of being able to control your thoughts more effectively. Plus, you control your emotional reaction to a given situation by controlling your thoughts. Yes, you might not be able to control the actions of others and the circumstances presented to you, however, you can control your thoughts. It is this control that keeps you from being a slave to your emotions, thus allowing you to act in a way that is in line with your values and goals.

4. See Criticism as Helpful

Criticism can be difficult to take, simply because it is an acknowledgement that we might not have done our best. Negative feedback can hurt; there is no question about that. It might not come with the best delivery, and that makes it even harder to take. Criticism can be even more difficult to take when it appears to be unfounded or coming from a misunderstanding. The benefit of emotional intelligence is that you take criticism, not as a character attack, but as a chance to learn and grow. Admittedly, that might not always be easy to do; however, it demonstrates a level of maturity in your character that allows you to grow and learn, even in the worst moments or when criticism is given in a blunt fashion.

At the same time, it can be easier to give criticism or praise, in a positive way, when you understand your emotions and how you can impact others' feelings. Being constructive in your criticism and praise, shows respect for others around you, and demonstrates your emotional maturity. It allows you to deepen your relationships with others, as they see you as someone who can respect and acknowledge their feelings.

5. Demonstrating Authenticity and Empathy

As I previously discussed authenticity, in Bedside Coaching #3, I just want to focus on how being able to handle and recognise your emotions, is critical to being true to your values and who you are as a person. It means saying what you mean, meaning what you say, and sticking to your values and principles above all else. Not everyone will appreciate what you share regarding your emotions, but it will help you to connect with those who appreciate your ability to share honestly.

Demonstrating empathy allows you to not only regulate your emotions but to acknowledge the emotions of others. It might mean showing support, even when the situation does not directly involve you. You are helping others through your empathy and the actions you take based on that.

6. Apologising Involves Forgive and Forget

When you apologise to others, you need to be humble enough to admit what you did to hurt them and be willing to acknowledge how your actions impacted them. It takes strength and courage to say that you are wrong and doing so can draw people to you. Forgiveness on your part also allows you to stop others from keeping you held hostage emotionally. Even if they have not apologised, forgiveness is about letting go and allowing yourself to move past those hurtful actions.

Your Coaching Task:

Take one of those areas above and explore it more fully through a journal. Think about instances where you have enjoyed that benefit, or where it was lacking. Part of the process is learning to evaluate your feelings and responses in a way that helps your emotional maturity to grow.

The Growth of Emotional Intelligence

Unlike many aspects of our physical self that we cannot change, such as our height for example, our emotional intelligence can grow and increase over time.

It is not always an easy process to control our emotions in a heated situation, or in the moments when we might feel disrespected by others, however, doing so can help you to manage the situation and your responses more effectively. It can help you to connect with others. In professional settings, your ability to lead can often be tied to your ability to handle your emotions and manage your reactions to the emotional responses of others.

Looking to find ways to grow your emotional intelligence? Book one of my free coaching sessions by visiting my website at **www.petrides.consulting**.

Readers Notes

Sophia Petrides

Readers Notes

Bedside Coaching #5 – Live Visual

For me, any coaching involves taking time to contemplate the changes that you want to make, and the process that you are undergoing to achieve them. However, this can be challenging if you are unclear about what you want in your life.

The process of determining what you want in your life, is the focus of this Bedside Coaching. Let's start by exploring visualisation, including what it is and how it can benefit you.

The Power and Beauty of Visualisation

You live in an amazing ball of energy, one that responds to how and what you think. Your thoughts are creative forces, and their expressions can be found in all aspects of your life. When you acknowledge that, you can begin to design the life that you want, with clarity and purpose.

Visualisation is the primary tool to assist you in that creation process. The beauty of this technique is that it helps you to map out your best and ideal life by accessing your subconscious and your imagination in a positive way. I love it, because visualisation is the way that you can build a mental picture of the life that you want to have.

Think of visualisation as a mental rehearsal of your life creation. Using it can be a powerful personal development tool, providing you the ability to get motivated. With the right use of this tool, you can create self-improvement, maintain good health, and much more. It helps you to focus and direct your thoughts. Part of the technique involves not just going through the process of visualising your ideal life just one time, it is about repeating the process on a regular basis. You have to see yourself being successful and achieving everything you have dreamed of.

Your Coaching Task:

Stop for a minute, close your eyes and take a few breaths to centre yourself. Be present in that moment and envision your best life. Give it as much detail as possible. If it helps, think of your life as a movie. Add the background, the foreground, and the various individuals that are part of your ideal life. Now that you have a clear picture, open your eyes and start to make notes about that vision.

Over the next few days, spend five minutes each day revisiting that vision of your ideal life. You may want to add more details and the point is to continue focusing on it and embedding it into your subconscious.

Your Focus is What You Attract

Part of the reason that daily visualisation is so powerful, can be attributed to the fact that it serves as a mental trick for your brain. Essentially, you are telling yourself that you already have what you desire. Doing so means that now you are in the position to engage your subconscious, getting it to act on your behalf.

Any situation that requires forethought and preparedness is going to involve using mental imagery. It doesn't matter if you are asking for a pay rise, delivering a speech, or speaking honestly to a loved one. All of these situations require you to spend time visualising and the results can be amazing, in terms of your ability to succeed.

You are drawing the creative powers of your thoughts into the mix. As your subconscious acts upon those images, you will begin to see its impact in your life. Now I want to be clear; this is not something that happens overnight. Instead, your persistence to keep the vision in your focus will help to keep your subconscious and thoughts engaged in achieving your life purpose and goals.

No matter what your definition of success looks like, you can achieve it. Visualisation is a way to get your thoughts lined up, and to open your mind to opportunities. When you are not focused, it can be hard to see the opportunities that are right in front of you. Instead, you tend to stop and start various goals with little progress made. At the end of those scattered efforts, you are left tired but with nothing to show for the energy expended.

Your Coaching Task:

Write a journal entry about moments in your life where you lacked focus. What was the outcome? How did you feel regarding the end result? It is important to recognise that the frustration and disappointment, which comes from not achieving the results you aimed for, are often a consequence of your lack of focus and vision.

Connecting to Your Life Purpose

Finding your purpose is going to be tied to what you focus on. Think about what you are passionate about and what brings you joy. Often, our purpose is tied to what motivates us to get up in the morning. Identifying, acknowledging and honouring that purpose is a critical part of the journey of successful individuals.

For some individuals, that purpose is obvious, based on their natural talents and skills. Others may find, identifying their purpose to be more challenging. The question on your mind might be how to clearly define your purpose. We are all born with a deep and meaningful purpose; however, it is up to us to discover what this is. Start with these two questions:

- What do you love doing?

- What comes easily to you?

Just because you might have a talent, does not mean that you are not going to have to work or practice hard. The point is that when you are developing a talent, it feels natural. Still, no matter how much work might be involved, you shouldn't feel as if you are suffering and struggling. If you feel that way, it is possible that you are not working toward achieving your purpose.

What qualities do you admire? Often, those qualities bring joy into your life when you express them. Focus on how you can make those qualities even more a part of your life, and you may be surprised how it translates into your purpose.

Finally, I want to spend some time focusing on your heart. It is the seat of motivation and can serve as your guidance system, telling you how to get from where you are, to your destination. The system doesn't work if you can't give it the end destination and the starting point. This means that it is important to decide where you want to go, even if you have not completely figured out your purpose.

That is why visualisation can be so important. It can help you to determine that end destination, even if you are not exactly sure how you are going to get there. Our next coaching task is going to focus on how to find that end destination.

Your Coaching Task:

You are going to create a life purpose statement. Start by envisioning your perfect world, where everyone is doing, being, and having everything that they want. Combine those three things into one statement, and that will give you a clear idea of what your purpose truly is.

Clarifying Your Life Purpose

Once you know what your purpose is, you need to keep focused on it constantly. It means setting goals that are in line with that purpose and being open to possibilities that can get you there much faster. Technology today has a way of connecting us with people and opportunities that can help us to accelerate achieving our purpose.

In the meantime, you need to look at all aspects of your life. Perhaps relationships within your inner circle are hindering your ability to reach your purpose. By working to address the problems within these relationships, you can break through these barriers. Be honest with yourself about the ways that you might be contributing to those obstacles, because doing so will help you to make changes and address the underlying issues.

Another point to consider in this process is the moments when you felt the most fulfilled. It can be from any period of time in your life. Why is this so important? Because when you feel fulfilled, then you are likely contributing to your growth and those around you.

By defining a few key moments when you felt fulfilled, you are likely going to notice that all those moments have something in common. It might be the service that you gave to others, or a sense of freedom. These positive patterns can be the neon arrows that help you define and clarify your purpose more fully.

Do not be quick to underestimate your purpose and what it can mean for others. My purpose involves helping others to grow and develop by making positive adjustments in their lives through coaching. I believe that it is a critical part of what I was meant to do. Now, everything that is a part of my life, including caring for myself and my relationships, is based around staying mentally and emotionally healthy to continue to fulfill my purpose.

In the midst of all that exploration and clarification of your purpose, through analysis of what fulfills you, there may also be patterns that are less positive, thus reflecting a lack of self-care. Part of the process of understanding yourself is wrapped up in the idea of self-care. After all, if you are neglected, then you are likely unable to engage in the type of self-awareness that is critical to your well-being. For more on self-awareness, I want to refer you back to Bedside Coaching #1.

With all of this information regarding your purpose, you might be excited to find it and pursue it. The problem, for many, is that this initial excitement gets drained by the world around us. Alternatively, you may find yourself struggling to stay motivated and positive as you head in the direction your journey was meant to take. Take advantage of one of my free coaching sessions and book a session with me today via my website, **www.petrides. consulting**.

That actually leads us to an important tool, one that is key to keeping you empowered and uplifted as you continue the process of growth and creation in your life.

Meditation: A Tool for Growth

Meditation is one of the critical aspects of mental health. I look at it as a means to process all of your life events and experiences, as well as your emotional responses. It is a way to keep up our motivation regarding our purpose. Our world is extremely busy and stressful. Every minute is full of a myriad of things demanding your attention. I have heard people talk about scheduling *me-time*, just to carve out time where they can just stop for a moment and focus on themselves.

It can be easy to get into a pattern where taking a few moments for yourself can seem impossible. After all, you are just trying to live your life and manage it. Yet in the midst of all that noise, you can lose your direction and be cut off from your vision of your ideal life.

Meditation is the way that you can reset and give your mind the quiet it needs to keep focusing on your vision and moving toward it. Taking a few minutes every day to quiet your mind and focus on your purpose and ideal life, is a way to reinforce your vision. It also provides you with the kind of motivation you need to keep moving forward, especially when you are dealing with different challenges from life.

Some very successful people use meditation because it allows the mind to clear and de-stress. Taking time to meditate daily can allow you to deal with your circumstances with a much clearer head, because you took time to pause, instead of reacting in the heat of the emotional moment, or focusing on the challenges instead of the potential solutions and opportunities that are right in front of you.

There are many meditation techniques available, and resources that go into much greater detail, but my purpose is to use it as a tool of calming, and allow it to help you refocus on the life you want to live, not the life you are living now.

Learning How to Meditate

You may now be sold on the idea of meditating, and you might be wondering how to do it. Meditation is like exercising your mental muscles. If you do not know how to do those exercises correctly, then you are not going to get as much benefit out of it. By learning the art of meditation, it can help you to exercise your mental and subconscious muscles, getting the most out of both.

Here are a few meditation techniques that can give you the tools to truly benefit from this process.

Sit for two minutes. It might seem like a small step, but I can tell you that once you carve out that first two minutes, it will get easier to grow that meditation time. During the two minutes, take deep breaths and focus on quieting your mind.

Make it part of your morning routine. When you wait until the end of the day, your mind will have been drained. It can make meditation difficult when your mind is whirring from daily events. Start your day with meditation to give yourself the benefit of a clear mind and heart before you begin your daily activities.

First focus on *doing*. Instead of trying to figure out if you are in the right position or sitting on the right cushion, focus on finding that quiet time in a place that is comfortable to you. It might be a favourite chair or corner of your garden. The point is to find quiet so that you can focus your mind and dwell on the thoughts that will positively impact your life.

Count your breaths! You may find it difficult to quiet your mind, and this technique might remind you of counting sheep in order to get to sleep. I want you to see it as a means of giving your mind a focus that pushes out other thoughts to the side. Counting is a way to quieten your mind, and that can be critical to the meditation process.

Wander with a loving attitude! Your thoughts are likely going to wander during meditation, and you might get off track. Even if you do, don't be too hard on yourself. Instead, gather your thoughts and start over. See the distracted thoughts as friends, instead of putting a negative connection to those wandering thoughts. It is not about being harsh; it is about demonstrating a loving attitude.

Stay with your thoughts and feelings! Spending time with those feelings and thoughts that might be uncomfortable can help you to learn more about yourself and contribute to your growth and power. You may notice that areas of your body can tighten up if you are dealing with a particularly stressful thought or feeling. Breathing and actively focusing on releasing that negativity can help you to move through it. At the same time, you are going to get into contact with your feelings and thoughts on a deeper level.

These are just a few of the ways that you can implement meditation in your daily routine. You do not have to be at home! If you are traveling in the morning, or dealing with a stressful situation at work, you can take a couple of minutes for meditation. The point is to work on making this mindfulness part of your daily routine and implementing it throughout your entire life.

Your Coaching Task:

Take two minutes every morning for meditation. Choose a particular aspect from one of the points above to focus on. You might also opt to meditate on your surroundings or how your body feels during this moment of quiet contemplation. Afterward, consider journaling about your feelings and what thoughts came up during the process.

Wrapping up Your Visualisation and Meditation

Throughout this Bedside Coaching, I have focused on the importance of visualisation and meditation. These two tools can help you to move through your journey of growth and creation, with greater support.

Visualisation does not have to be limited to your mental picture. You can use physical pictures, drawings, and boards to create a physical manifestation of your vision.

Doing so can help you to maintain your focus, especially when you get distracted by circumstances in your life. Part of this process goes beyond creating a vision and meditation.

After all, even if you know where you are going, you still need that GPS to give you the step-by-step instructions to get there. These tools are part of the process when it comes to achieving your goals, which is the focus of your next Bedside Coaching.

Sophia Petrides

Readers Notes

Readers Notes

Sophia Petrides

Readers Notes

.

Bedside Coaching #6 – Live Goals

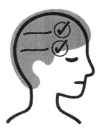

One of my passions in life is to scuba dive, as I love being in the ocean and exploring the depths of our beautiful and mystical blue planet.

I was once told that I would not be able to dive, as I did not have a big enough lung capacity. I also suffer from asthma, which seemed to be the medical nail in the coffin. Stubborn as I am when I want to achieve something, my medical situation did not deter me from reaching my goal. Instead, I started training hard in order to get myself fit enough to pass the Advanced Padi Dive Certification. Since then, I have enjoyed diving in some of the most beautiful sites in the world, including the Great Barrier Reef. To date, I have logged 90 dives.

I would never have reached this point without setting myself goals. Over and over again, I set various milestones that led me to be strong enough and having enough lung capacity to complete my scuba dives.

Setting goals is a way to help you really commit to yourself! In your mind and heart, you are locking into a journey meant to end in personal growth and blessings. When I was determined to scuba dive, I focused on the end goal and put milestones or smaller goals into place. As I achieved each of those smaller goals, I set myself up for success. That larger goal kept getting closer with each step. So, let's get started by understanding why goals are so important, and how you can create your own goals. Keep that journal handy, because much of what you need is likely already woven into your writing and thought process to date.

Why Set Goals?

The importance of goals cannot be understated. Humans are notorious procrastinators. We need deadlines and goals to help keep us on track. Being committed to the process means finding ways to stay engaged. Goals are a way to do that.

Here are a few reasons for setting goals and why they are so critical to your success:

1. *They propel you into growth.* When you have a goal written down, with a set date to have it accomplished, you have an external representation of your internal desires. It reminds you about what you want to achieve. Goals can also help you to stay connected and motivated to achieve those inner desires, especially during those times when your focus and energy might be at a low ebb.

2. *They transform mountains into hills.* Have you ever wanted to make a significant change, however, the idea of that change seemed overwhelming? Goals are a way to break larger aspirations into stepping stones that can be easier to achieve. As you achieve those smaller goals, then you are moving toward the achievement of

that larger challenging goal. Now you have a definitive plan of action and a source of real motivation. It will help you to be happier through the journey of creation in your life.

3. *They create a belief in what you are capable of accomplishing.* When you set goals and achieve them, it gives you a source of confidence and helps you to believe in yourself. You now know what you can achieve, and that can fuel your ambition. At the same time, if you aren't achieving your goals, then it can help you to isolate the ways and areas where you need to make real changes to get on track.

4. *They help you to see what you really want.* Goals might not always reflect what you want, but if you don't set them, you won't be able to test what is or isn't right for you. Constantly reassessing your goals gives you the benefit of introspection and self-reflection. Once you figure out what you really want, then you can go out and make it happen.

Without a question, goals help us to live our best life, because they push us to grow and continually improve. How can you implement goal setting into your life, especially now that you have a vision of the life you want to have?

Using a Visualisation Board and Affirmations

In Bedside Coaching #5, I discussed the importance of using visualisation. In that coaching chapter, I wanted you to create a mental picture. Now let's focus on bringing that mental image into your physical reality.

Visualisation boards are a way to do that. You are affirming what you want to create in your life and display it on a board. Your board should include pictures, words, and other elements that bring your mental picture to life. Why is it so critical to give yourself a reinforcement of your vision?

To affirm something is to confirm that it is true. When it comes to your ideal life, an affirmation is a statement of truth to absorb and make a part of your reality. They are not just wishful thinking; they are dynamic and practical. They work in part because they are based upon higher truths, known as the Law of Attraction.

Affirmations give you the power to change! Identify your affirmations through your visionary board, and then repeat them consistently in your daily life. Your brain simply acts as if they have already happened or exist, bringing them into your reality.

Creating a visionary board can help you to enrich your vision with all the detail to make it vivid in your subconscious and conscious mind. Craft affirmations that work in harmony with your vision. I suggest you jot these down on 3x5 cards and keep them by your bed. Read them first thing in the morning and last thing at night.

Using repetition, you ingrain those affirmations into your mind, allowing them to influence you to change your habits and patterns. Give yourself control through affirmations that help you to target and focus your thoughts effectively.

Here are just a few examples of affirmations. You can create your own custom ones to reflect what you want and need in your life.

- I will love others as extensions of my own self and of the love that I feel from above.

- My actions now will create a new and better future for others, one filled with inner joy and peace.

Both focus not just on you but on how you can impact others. The "bigger picture" expands beyond just your immediate wants and needs. It needs to be greater to have a truly fulfilling effect in your life, and to draw you closer to your purpose.

Avoid writing negative words or phrases into your affirmations. Good affirmations are positive and will affirm positive qualities. Another tip is to make sure that you phrase your affirmations in the present tense. If you are not sure what to put into your affirmations or how to phrase them, coaching can give you some guidance

Your Coaching Task:

Purchase a board or cardboard paper and start creating your visionary board. Include pictures, quotes, and phrases that compliment your vision. Look at it daily! Another aspect of this task is to create affirmations of your own, following the guidelines in this section. Remember, the point is to keep you focused on your goals.

Creating Your Goals for the Next 3 to 5 Years

Now that you have a vision and understand the importance of setting goals, we need to create your big goals. Start by envisioning the next three to five years. In the below space, I want you to write out your long-term goals. Be clear about what you want, and then think about whether they are aligned with your vision of your ideal life.

Sophia Petrides

Readers Goals

Readers Goals

Now that you have set the goals, it is time to start breaking them down into the milestones that you are going to be able to achieve, over the coming weeks and months.

Set Your Short-Term Goals

Achieving your long-term goals involves achieving short-term goals. Now that you have identified those long-term goals, we need to break them down even further. Your short-term goals could be what you want to accomplish in the next week or the next month. The point of these goals is that they move you closer to achieving your long-term goals.

All of these goals are going to benefit you in terms of keeping your motivation high, because you will be moving forward. Plus, you are setting timelines, which are critical to achieving goals, big and small. A goal with no timeframe is a goal that will not be accomplished.

Opportunities for growth come from achieving goals. You will be in a different place in one year, three years, and five years, because of these smaller goals that you set and completed. If you want to create change in your life, then you need to start with setting those goals.

In this section, I want you to start writing out those small goals. I have included a few blank pages for you to note these down. Be specific and include timeframes.

Readers Short-Term Goals

Sophia Petrides

Readers Short-Term Goals

Now that you have set your goals, it is time to start talking about what often blocks us from making major changes in our lives. It is the power of fear, which is the topic of my next Bedside Coaching.

Sophia Petrides

Readers Notes

Bedside Coaching #7 – Live Fearless

The world is geared to make us afraid in every aspect of our lives. Just think about the daily news. There are stories about people being hurt doing normal, everyday activities; political and social upheavals that alter people's lives; and the impact of natural disasters.

Each of these stories builds on the next, creating a culture of fear that contributes to a high level of panic and anxiety, even if you are not actually being impacted negatively or are in any real danger. Over time, those levels of anxiety can only allow fear to build and reach the point where they can become paralyzing.

No matter where you look, society is telling you to be cautious, to be suspicious, and by default to be fearful. Today, so many of us opt out of making amazing choices or taking advantage of opportunities, because of fear. There is the fear of failure, the fear of shame, the fear of physical harm, the fear of damaging relationships, the fear of rejection, the fear of loss of approval, or the fear of loss. No matter what the fear, it ends up blocking us from receiving the benefits that come with stepping out and taking a chance.

Fear is normal. It is part of our psychological nature to help us avoid dangerous situations. It can serve a purpose to keep us safe and alive. However, the problem comes when we allow the emotions associated with fear to overtake us and make us anxious and extremely fearful. What has happened is that our culture has fostered a fear of *fear*!

As a result, we can allow fear to overwhelm its natural boundaries that provide protection, and instead, allow ourselves to end up stuck in various areas of our lives. That fear drives us to protect ourselves from dangers that are not really dangers at all or have a significantly small likelihood of occurring.

Again, it is that fear, and the anxiety that it produces, that ends up creating a paralyzing effect in your life.

When we talked about self-awareness, in Bedside Coaching #1, I focused specifically on techniques that would allow you to learn more about who you are and what your purpose in life is.

Now I want you to use that self-awareness to start identifying how fear could be impacting your life and blocking your path. You need to find a way to first identify what you fear, then define the beliefs behind the fears, and take control back from those fears.

First, let's start with defining your fears and how they are impacting your life. After all, you cannot change what you do not know or have not acknowledged. Once you have the knowledge, then you can start making the progress that will allow you to make significant changes and shifts to take your life in a new direction.

Your Coaching Task:

Take a piece of paper or a page in your journal and write down the fears that you may have encountered throughout the day. It could have been a fear related to your professional life, or it could have been a fear related to your personal relationships. I want you to now take a few moments to meditate on a few of those fears. Ask yourself:

- What choices did I make or not make based on that fear?

- What were the consequences from that choice or lack of a choice?

The point of this task is to start thinking about how your fears are impacting your life, in ways both large and small.

Defining the Beliefs Behind Your Fears

Now that you have an understanding of what your fears are, it is time to start diving into the beliefs that underlie those fears. It can be easy to look at a fear and assign it a simple surface reason that motivates it. The reality is that many of our fears actually are based on long-held beliefs about ourselves, and how we relate to others and the world around us.

For instance, you may have been raised in a household where your parents dealt with a large degree of loss, perhaps financially. It coloured how they thought about money. Your parents might have been quick to squirrel away cash, and found it difficult to spend money, fearing what would happen if they did. That attitude and belief system may have been passed on to you. Now let's think about how that could have negatively impacted your finances.

You might have been less inclined to take risks in your professional life, because you didn't want to risk the paycheck that you knew you already had coming in. The idea of taking on a new assignment, or even going into business for yourself, could have felt too risky and dangerous, and therefore triggered your fear response. Those opportunities closed, and you did not take advantage of them for fear of losing what you already had financially. Your belief system fed a fear that stopped you from potentially moving forward to greater financial gains.

This is just one example of how your beliefs can feed your fears. As your fears grow, they take on more of an influence in your life, to the point that they begin to control the decisions you make and determine the risks that you are unwilling to take in your professional and personal lives.

The point in this Bedside Coaching is to acknowledge how your fears may have grown, but also to understand how you reached the point that those fears are now blocking opportunities. As you reflect on your fears from the first coaching task, I want you to keep in mind that fear can be healthy, but when you give it the power and control, then it can impede your ability to grow as a person.

Fear can end up invading your internal dialogue and focus you on a negative thought pattern. Once you start this negative pattern, you then begin to create the internal loop that feeds your negative thinking and your fear at the same time.

Part of engaging with and addressing your fears involves acknowledging that you can feel fear and still move forward. Doing so allows you to develop courage, which is not the absence of fear but recognising the fear and moving through it anyway. You can use your courage to help you control your response to what scares you. Once you do so, it leaves you feeling empowered!

Your Coaching Task:

Now that you have a list of your fears, it is important to start unpacking the reasons and beliefs that feed these fears. Take one or two fears from your list and think about past experiences related to these. Write them down. Then ask yourself:

- What do these experiences have in common?

- What did they teach me to fear?

- How have I allowed these experiences to colour my beliefs and choices?

Determining why you have a fear, and the deeper meaning behind it, can be difficult, but through meditation and effort, you can begin the process of addressing what beliefs and experiences are contributing to your fears.

Changing Beliefs to Conquer Your Fears

Now that you understand what your fears are and have a deeper understanding of what is behind these, it is time to start shifting your beliefs to address those fears. I am talking about giving yourself the power to stand up and take chances. If you know that certain beliefs are holding you back, it is important to start changing your internal dialogue that feeds the beliefs.

Part of this process will involve writing down those beliefs and then writing down an alternative belief, the one that you hope to adopt. Once you do so, it is important to consciously make that new belief part of your mental dialogue. Repeating it on a daily basis will help your subconscious begin to make a shift that alters your thinking. It is not an easy process, and it does take time. One of the things that can help the process is to meditate on times that you took risks and stood up to your fears.

How did those experiences end? Were your fears justified? Often, when we look back at those experiences, we find ourselves actually remembering a feeling of confidence or even joy at our success. I want you to make it a habit to recall those moments, allowing that confidence to help you to address and conquer other fears. It will not be an easy process, but with determination, you can conquer your fears!

As part of the process of changing your beliefs, you are also going to be addressing other areas of your life. It can be hard to imagine how many opportunities you have missed because you let your beliefs create the fears that held you back.

Once you find yourself conquering those fears, you can use those experiences to help you recognise when a fear could be blocking you or even causing you to act in an irrational manner. When you can control your response to what scares you, it gives you the power to do what you want, and to conquer new challenges and explore new experiences.

Part of the reason that I wanted to address this in *Bedside Coaching* is because I recognise that fears can keep you from doing what you dream with your life. It could be a fear of a lack of financial security, or a fear of losing relationships, or a fear of losing professional status by moving in a new direction. When those fears take over your life, then you do not know what you might have accomplished, and you end up living with a lifetime of regrets.

Do I believe that every time you take a risk or conquer a fear to explore an opportunity that it will be successful? The reality is that you are not going to find success every time.

However, even failures can be opportunities to learn and grow. Therefore, it is important to adjust how you view failing. Instead of using it to feed your fears, allow it to help you grow and open your mind to new ways of doing things and other opportunities.

Your Coaching Task:

Take one or two beliefs and rewrite them to help them feed your courage instead of your fear. Ask yourself:

- What about this belief empowers me?

- If it doesn't empower me, then how can I adjust my belief to empower myself?

When you open your mind and show a willingness to change your beliefs, you empower yourself to change your life.

The Challenge is to Take a Risk

According to Merriam-Webster Dictionary, courage is defined as a *"mental or moral strength to venture, persevere and withstand danger, fear, or difficulty."* Part of conquering your fear means developing your personal and mental courage. It is a mental muscle, and one that you need to use, in order for it to develop.

Think about all the muscles in your body. Perhaps you do a job that is physically demanding, and so you have developed muscles in certain areas, perhaps your back or your arms. Now they may stand out, but it is because they have been worked more consistently. Yet you could develop other muscles in your body if you are willing to put in the time and energy to train and build them up. Courage is just another type of muscle, one that needs to be put to use so that you can develop it over time.

How can you develop courage? As I already mentioned, changing your beliefs is an important part of conquering your fears, but at a certain point, you are simply going to have to do what you are afraid of, and then experience the results of taking that leap. I understand that it may not be easy, because you are going against everything that your belief system and internal dialogue says is a bad idea, even dangerous.

Yet if you do not take those initial steps by taking a risk, you will spend your life remaking beliefs without allowing them to help you remake your life. Even if you change a belief, it will not positively impact your life's course if you do not allow that new belief to influence your actions and choices. Note that I am talking about taking action, and thus building new experiences on which you can base your adjusted beliefs.

Courage comes when you see yourself acting in spite of a fear or negative belief. When you are working on developing your courage, don't take a big leap at first. You might want to start with a smaller risk or a fear that doesn't bring high levels of anxiety with it. When you are successful in taking that risk, then you start to build a pattern of experiences that you can draw on to give you courage in situations where the stakes are much higher.

After all, working out one time doesn't mean that you can now bench over 500 pounds. It takes time to build your strength, and building your courage happens in much the same way. Essentially, every successful experience of overcoming a fear builds a foundation for your courage, one that you can use to support taking bigger risks for greater opportunities and amazing life experiences.

Your Coaching Task:

Take a risk, even if it is a small one. Write down how you felt about the experience. Ask yourself:

- What did you learn about your abilities?

- How did taking this risk help you to grow, either personally or professionally?

- Even if you weren't successful, did the consequences you feared materialise?

Every risk that you take can support you to develop your courage and allow you to make the changes to redirect your life. It is not about getting rid of fear but learning to act in spite of your fears.

If you are trying to determine your next steps in the face of your fears, visit my website at **www.petrides.consulting** to book one of my free coaching sessions. Let's work on it together!

Understanding When Your Fears
May Have Become Irrational

I want to address this because many of us have unreasonable fears, ones that can bring paralyzing anxiety along with them. We imagine the consequences of taking that risk to be so damaging and horrific, and it can cause a level of panic so great, that we essentially freeze up.

I think of these as our irrational fears, simply because the basis of these fears are not realistic, however, our minds have fixated on them for so long that they have become giants in our world.

Have you ever had one of these paralyzing fears? By working through your previous coaching tasks, you may have begun to identify what is behind these fears and you may be unable to overcome the fear itself. As you develop your courage, you also need to give yourself some tools to address irrational fears.

Start by asking yourself these two questions:

1. What is the absolute worst that can happen?

2. If the worst happened, how would you be impacted?

Many times, the worst is wrapped up in how people see us. Our sense of self could be wrapped up in others to an unhealthy degree, allowing us to build up irrational fears and worries. You might fixate on it so much that you build up the situation to being something even worse in your mind. The point of these questions is not about dismissing the fear. Instead, I want you to be able to rein in your fixation on the fear and those imagined consequences.

Once you are able to bring them back down to earth, it can be easier to address them and manage them. As you build your courage, you may also find yourself opening up to the idea of conquering these fears. Along the way, I want you to also build up your tool chest for dealing with anxiety. Fear and anxiety can be paralyzing to the point that it stops us from living the best life possible.

With this coaching chapter, I hope I have helped you to recognise some of your fears and also given you tools to address them. If you have a long list of fears, do not labour under the belief that you have to conquer them all at once. In fact, I encourage you to just work on one or two at a time.

Motivation comes from achieving a goal. It makes you want to achieve more and conquering your fears can work in much the same way. Therefore, make it a point to document this journey so that you can begin to build up that motivation and inspiration from what you have already achieved, to conquer even more in the future.

Your Coaching Task:

Identify two fears that you want to address. Work through the coaching steps in this chapter. Write down how you felt as you faced that fear and walked through it. Make sure that you focus on what you were thinking, the decisions you made, and how you felt during and after the process.

Doing so will give you a source of inspiration to tackle another fear and take a greater risk that will lead to a significant change in your life!

Sophia Petrides

Readers Notes

Readers Notes

Sophia Petrides

Readers Notes

Bedside Coaching – "Your Legacy"

To create an amazing life, one that lets you grow constantly and to support achieving your dreams, you need to step beyond your own life and consider how you can impact others. Often, the greatest thing we can do for ourselves is to reach out to others, supporting them to follow in our footsteps and grow themselves.

Our life purpose is wrapped up in the ability to take our wisdom and experience, sharing them with the next generation, be it through your passion or vision for change. However, you might be struggling to define your life purpose, or wonder if you even have one. I want to focus on how you can recognise your life purpose and then begin to work toward it.

First, as you have gone through the various *Bedside Coaching* chapters, you have likely gotten a deeper understanding of who you are and what drives, motivates, and inspires you. That type of journey involved a level of honesty and open mindedness. However, do not think that your journey is over. In fact, you have just begun your journey toward building and change. Now let's turn our attention to something that I believe is greater than our individual journey, and that is what we can do for others.

Creating a Legacy to Empower Others

You might have found your purpose and be very active in making it happen. Your thoughts and subconscious are working in harmony. Your reality has begun to match that original vision that you had for your ideal life.

There are many individuals who achieve what they believe to be their passion, based on what motivates them, only to find that it is not the entire journey. Remember when we talked about finding your purpose? You envisioned what a perfect world looks like and then narrowed it down to yourself.

Now you need to revisit that vision and note how your actions and thoughts are impacting others. In that vision of the perfect world, you saw others doing, being, and enjoying their best lives.

Your legacy is to help others walk the path that leads them to achieving their best life, just as you have already done. That might not be easy, but it is a critical part of expanding your purpose to impact the next generation.

The remainder of your life purpose involves how to take your gift, talents, and abilities to the next level, creating a legacy that can be passed to others. It can involve providing coaching for others, motivating them by sharing your life experiences and what you have learned from them. It is not easy to take your purpose to this level; however, it is critical to feel complete and whole.

Your ideal life is one that includes your life purpose and addresses all aspects of your personal and professional self. How can you take that and transform it into a purpose that impacts others?

Building a Powerful Legacy for Others

Part of this journey involves recognising what it takes to build a powerful legacy. Your life is an amazing adventure, one that can have a powerful impact on others. What are you doing when you make the biggest difference in someone's life? Do more of that!

Be joyful! You serve as an example to others, and when you serve others with joy, then you spread that joy around. Don't wait for the perfect time, because it will never come. Create the perfect time right now!

Life is a journey that travels far too quickly. I encourage you to build a legacy of doing what matters now, and modeling that for others. Let them see you engaging in the now, instead of putting it off for tomorrow. You will be amazed at how much change you can create simply by getting started.

If you think that everything you do in service of others needs to be a huge event, then you are missing the point. Small opportunities to be kind and serve, happen every day. Seize them and start making a difference today. You never know if those big opportunities are being signaled by the small ones right in front of you.

Often, those small opportunities involve those individuals you are closest to. I believe that service starts in your own garden, and then you can branch out. When you bring your best self to your personal and professional lives, then you are able to create and connect in a deeper and more meaningful way.

If your focus is building a legacy, then you will not be successful. Instead, make your focus about serving others and elevating their needs above your own. Reaching out, even when it is not the easiest thing to do, can be the way to make the biggest difference.

As you work to serve others, it is important to eliminate those behaviours and attitudes that will dilute the impact of your service. You might be building positive behaviours and actions into your life, but that is not enough. Focus on eliminating the negative behaviours and actions that are impacting you and others around you.

When you look at the coaching lessons throughout this book, there are plenty of positive things that you can do and focus on. Many of them are meant to replace a negative aspect in your life. You can't bring your best self to anything if you are not actively digging out the negative and encouraging the growth of your positive traits.

Throughout this journey, you have the opportunity to make choices to turn from anger, hate, judgement and fear, toward love, hope, and joy. Do not allow the urgencies of life to smother your priorities!

You are building a solid foundation, and it starts by being aware of the value you bring to others. If you believe compassion is what makes life better, then be an example of acting with compassion daily. There are moments when we can show compassion and kindness to others, in ways large and small.

Doing so, will also help you to see the needs of those around you. After all, your talents and abilities can help others, but only if you know how to use them to impact that community and meet those needs. Ask yourself, "What can I give that the world needs?" You might be surprised by the answer to that question.

I have continued to focus on writing, particularly in a journal. It is a great way to get your thoughts out of your head and to stop the circle of negativity. Use your writing to get things off your chest, even if you cannot give them a voice in any other setting.

There are a variety of opportunities available, so use journaling to open your mind and heart to the possibilities.

Everyone brings assets and virtues to the community. Match those assets with your values, and then use those tools to help others. If you knew that you only had a few years left, how would you want to spend them? What do you want others to remember about you and how you lived your life?

Determine what is going to be your primary focus, and do not allow the small things to distract you from that focus. Maybe this means simplifying your life to give you the energy to build connections with others. Put the bulk of your energy into those activities that are your priorities and let go of the rest.

We are all creating legacies, even if we are not actively thinking about it. The question is whether we are creating the legacy that we want to leave to others. Are you living your life in a way that you want to be remembered for, or are you living a life that is dictated by others and lacks authenticity? If you build a powerful legacy, then your impact can be felt across generations.

Lead a deliberate life, one where you focus on doing the right thing with kindness and a joyful spirit.

Starting today, you are in the legacy building business. Go out there and create!

Sophia Petrides

Readers Notes

Readers Notes

Sophia Petrides

Readers Notes

Bedside Coaching – Wrap Up

Throughout this book, my goal has been to share tools, techniques and teachings that can help you to empower yourself to create. There are so many of us that get stuck in our heads or in circumstances that are limiting. Once we get stuck, the idea of creating change can be fearful, almost too scary to contemplate.

Some of us have been stuck, however, there are so many of us that have become unstuck because we reclaimed our power. I wanted you to have the ability to get moving, empower, and motivate yourself to fulfill your purpose. You are building a cooperation internally so that you stop getting in your own way.

Coaching is part of my life because I enjoy serving others to find both their personal and professional paths and build upon these paths, to create their ideal life. That is not easy to do on your own. We get stuck in our own ways, lacking motivation and inspiration, and it becomes like New Year's resolutions that are quickly forgotten or abandoned.

Part of what coaching brings to you is a level of accountability that you cannot provide for yourself. Let's face it, you have likely made multiple excuses throughout your life for why you haven't achieved what you wanted; aren't as successful as you want to be and haven't created this ideal life you have been dreaming of. Those excuses are roadblocks and working with a coach helps you to blast them apart and get moving again.

Throughout each of these coaching sessions, I wanted you to get a small task to complete. After all, the way you eat an elephant is one bite at a time. If you set large goals for yourself, those goals can get overwhelming and leave you in a position where you just want to give up.

As a coach, I work in partnership with you and along the way, I keep you empowered, motivated and inspired to achieving your goals timely. I get you to focus on the bite in front of you, instead of the whole elephant. Once you tackle that first bite, then you can start the next one. Milestones are a great way to tackle larger goals and to create growth.

Often, what motivates us is signs of progress in our lives. That progress is key to everything! No matter what you do, progress is what keeps you moving through the challenges, the obstacles, and the struggles to make it to the opportunities, the open doors, and your ideal life.

Everything begins with a thought, so it is important to be mindful of what you are thinking about and focusing on. You are in control of your thoughts, so empower yourself on a daily basis through the various coaching lessons in this book. It is amazing what you can create once you put your mind, consciousness and thoughts to work for you, instead of dwelling on the negative that keeps you chained in a place that is not benefiting you.

You might be at the point that you are ready for a coach, because you have made it as far as you can on your own. My coaching services are focused on helping you to take those next steps on your journey that can keep you moving toward your ideal life. Remember that you are always in a state of learning, but only if you allow your mind to be open to the process.

Time and again, I work with individuals who need that outside point of view to help them get moving and reclaim their focus. These individuals are looking to create change in their professional life; along the way, they gather skills and tools to address issues or difficulties in their personal life.

Another aspect of coaching is helping you to mature emotionally, giving you the tools to lead others, while understanding how you can positively impact your relationships. You are working to better yourself, and along the way, others will benefit from your example.

My advice is simple! Start at the beginning by reading just a small portion; then take a few minutes every day to focus on that. It means clearing your mind and allowing yourself to just focus on that small section. As you move from chapter to chapter, take advantage of those "Readers Notes" pages to document your thoughts or points that stand out.

Look for ways to apply what you are learning in your daily life. It might be possible to find specific moments or instances where you can implement what you are learning. As these lessons become a part of your normal, you can continue to expand into other *Bedside Coaching* chapters.

Being honest with yourself and analyzing your own actions is not easy. If it were, then all of us would be taking this journey of empowerment. Instead, you will be uncomfortable at various points. I want you to see how, even in the most difficult aspects of your journey, there is a benefit.

Focusing on how you are learning and growing, even during the challenging times, you are coming to a deeper understanding of yourself and your mindset. Thus, it allows you to become more appreciative and grateful for everything in your life.

If you are interested in individual coaching, please contact me through **www.petrides.consulting**. I also encourage you to explore my retreats and masterclass seminars, where you can network with other likeminded individuals who are looking to create change in their own lives.

May you find peace and growth in your journey!

About the Authors

Sophia Petrides

Sophia is an author, professional development coach and personal branding consultant, supporting her clients to achieve realistic personal and career goals and become more effective in their day-to-day business. Sophia does this by helping them express and enhance important personal values like integrity, creativity, openness, and authenticity.

Sophia has enjoyed a successful and rewarding career in the corporate events industry, with an impressive track record that reflects a wide range of senior roles and functions within the sector. Sophia has come to view the events industry as a dynamic business ecosystem that builds long-lasting relationships between the brands, senior executives, and clients. Working within leading investment banks— such as Credit Suisse, Barclays Capital, Barclays Wealth, BNP Paribas, and most recently, with leading global events agency, FIRST—her work has often gravitated toward senior management functions, structuring events, roadshows, and hospitality teams for Goldman Sachs, PIMCO, and Deutsche Bank. These roles supported her clients to deliver consistently best-in-class engagements for corporate institutions and high net-worth clients.

Sophia passionately believes that we are all more than just a CV. As we mature professionally, we develop a personal brand that makes us stand out as individuals; however, we are often not fully aware of what our unique assets and values are.

As a coach, she offers a holistic approach to companies that need their employees to grow dynamically, improving KPI performance and delivering outstanding ROI through goal-oriented personal development plans. Sophia focuses on work-life balance, building resilience and stress management techniques, and helping individuals define their personal brand in terms of where they want to be career-wise and in their personal lives... and how to get there.

Sophia sees her role as a partner who enables a "bigger picture" for individuals and teams, namely the idea that developing positive workplaces—with happy employees—enables effective change management, improves talent acquisition, and strengthens talent retention that drives continuous business growth.

Sophia's track record as an intuitive, confident team leader has helped her evolve a creative coaching method that sets ambitious personal and professional goals, and helps teams achieve them.

She currently resides in the United Kingdom and travels frequently around the globe for both work and leisure.

To book one of Sophia's free sample coaching sessions, connect with her at **www.petrides.consulting**.

Raymond Aaron

Raymond Aaron is a New York Times Top 10 bestselling author, investor, business owner and internationally renowned thought leader and success coach. His techniques have generated over $160,000,000.00 from the sale of products and services and over 1100 investment properties valued over $500,000,000.00.

Raymond Aaron, has committed his life to teaching people how to dramatically change their lives for the better. Raymond transforms lives by helping people tap into their own potential.

Today, Raymond is helping people achieve greater wealth, branding, recognition, confidence, respect and authority. Raymond teaches his clients how to become respected authorities and experts in their fields.

Raymond has shared his vision and wisdom on radio and television programs. He is the author of 8 best-selling books, including "Branding Small Business For Dummies," "Double Your Income Doing What You Love" and the co-author of New York Times best-seller "Chicken Soup for the Parent's Soul" and author of the Canadian best-seller, "Chicken Soup for the Canadian Soul." He is also an avid adventurer having completed one of the world's toughest races, Polar Race (a 350 mile foot race to the Magnetic North Pole).

Testimonials

"If you want to be guaranteed a good night's sleep and wake up refreshed in the morning, I recommend this book as the best tonic. You will find yourself ready to tackle your personal self-help journey."

Ronel Lehmann, Founder and Chief Executive,
Finito Education Ltd.

"There are two things that make Bedside Coaching stand out from the other self-help books in this area. Firstly, it is designed to sit by your bed and provide accessible insights into how to progress your life goals. This means you learn something useful just before you fall asleep, which helps your unconscious mind digest it and store it in your memory. Secondly, each chapter is broken into bite size chunks with a range of practical exercises— from 5-minute visualisation tasks to keeping a daily diary of progress—in a particular area of your personal or work life. These are easy exercises (designed for time-poor busy people like me) that transform the ideas in the book into practical thinking habits. These two strengths of the book combine to make Bedside Coaching feel like a personalised coaching programme for maintaining healthier attitudes to work, stress, home life, and all those tricky bits in-between."

Andrew Keith Walker,
Technology Writer and Broadcaster

"I have known Sophia for over 15 years and did recruit her into a senior management role at FIRST Global Events Agency, in 2012. As a company that was accredited with Investor in People Gold and reached No.14 in the 2017 Great Place to Work rankings, a massive strategic focus was on our culture, our talent management, and our people development. Sophia played a crucial leadership role in recruiting the best talent, coaching high-performance, and building strategic personal development programmes that both retained and advanced that talent. Sophia's strong emotional intelligence, insightful intuition, and positive presence make for a solid and reliable coach, able to guide and inspire future senior leaders. Not only would I happily work with Sophia again, we are still in regular contact where I call upon her counsel and sound good advice."

Mark Riches – Advisor,
NED and SME Investor

"Last year, I set up my Management Consulting business in Vienna. In the early stages, Sophia supported me in creating my visionary board and defining my values on which my business was based upon. In her authentic way, Sophia coached me by challenging me to find creative solutions and to set clear goals, which have supported me in finding the space and time in my very busy professional and personal life, to stay focused and manage the various challenges of setting up a new business effectively. Even though I am based in Vienna, it was a new experience for me to be coached via FaceTime; however, we both built a very good rapport, and I was very happy with the outcome for each of our sessions. Thank you very much Sophia for empowering me!"

Caroline Hahn,
Management Consultant (Vienna)

Testimonials

"Sophia is a force of nature! I had the luck to be coached by Sophia on several occasions. She is naturally non-judgemental and caring, and she brings all of her experience and wisdom to every session. I value her perspective on things, which is almost never what you would anticipate!"

Peter Knupffer,
Professional Co-active Coach to Changemakers

"I can truly say that Sophia is an experienced coach that has the innate ability to connect with people. She is warm and charismatic, and supported me in seeing things from a different perspective. Her energy, experience, and leadership skills added an additional dimension to our coaching sessions—she was able to challenge with a great deal of empathy. I learned a lot from our sessions and have taken away insight and tools that have supported in both my personal and professional growth."

Jemma Matthews,
Senior Human Resources Professional

"It gives me great pleasure to be writing a recommendation for Sophia, whom I have known for over 20 years. I first met Sophia when I was put in charge of Global Events for Credit Suisse First Boston, in 1997. She demonstrated a high level of client service, and I knew immediately that with her attention to detail, high level of client service, and industry network, she would be a great asset to the EMEA events team in London. Since that time, we have worked together in many different roles; and when I joined Barclays Investment Bank as the Global Head of Events and Roadshows, in 2005, I immediately offered Sophia the role of EMEA Head of Events. Sophia has been a role model, coach and mentor for many successful event planners over the years, at both Credit Suisse and Barclays. She is an expert in the industry and respected by senior management for her ability to build strong relationships and be results driven. She has a wealth of knowledge and experience to share in her coaching career!"

Alex Oakes – Managing Director,
Global Event & Roadshow Marketing

"I have known Sophia for over 20 years and we have worked together at Credit Suisse, Barclays Capital, and most recently, at FIRST in partnership with Goldman Sachs. During this time, she has inspired and motivated her teams to be one of the best in the industry, by coaching, mentoring, and retaining talent. With her knowledge and experience, she has an incredible ability to build strong relationships with her team, clients, and key stakeholders."

Lisa Simmons – Senior Events Consultant

Visit my website **www.petrides.consulting**
to book one of my free sample coaching sessions today!

Printed in Poland
by Amazon Fulfillment
Poland Sp. z o.o., Wrocław

54746411R00083